Political and Economic Systems
COMMUNISM

David Downing

Heinemann Library
Chicago, Illinois

© 2008 Heinemann Library
a division of Reed Elsevier Inc.
Chicago, Illinois

Customer Service 888-454-2279
Visit our website at www.heinemannraintree.com

Designed by Richard Parker and Q2A Creative
Illustrations: Art Construction
Printed and bound in Hong Kong

12 11 10 09 08
10 9 8 7 6 5 4 3 2 1

New edition ISBN: 978-1-4329-0232-2 (hardcover)
                   978-1-4329-0757-0 (paperback)

**The Library of Congress has catalogued the first
edition as follows:**
Downing, David, 1946 Aug. 9-
     Communism / David Downing.
         p. cm. -- (Political and economic systems)
Includes bibliographical references and index.
     ISBN 1-40340-316-3
     1. Communism -- Juvenile literature.
     [1. Communism] I. Title. II. Series.
     HX21 .D693 2003
     335.43--dc21

                         2002006317

Acknowledgments
The publishers would like to thank the following for permission to reproduce photographs:
Corbis/Bettmann: pp. 17, 32, 46; Corbis/David and Peter Turnley: p. 55; Corbis/Hulton-
Deutsch Collection p. 37; David King Collection: pp. 24, 33; Getty Images/Keystone p.27;
Getty Images/Hulton: pp. 7, 9, 13, 16, 22, 39, 41, 43; Masterfile/Wei Yan: p. 48; Novosti:
pp. 10, 19, Popperfoto: pp. 23, 28, 44, 53; Popperfoto/Darren Whiteside Reuters: p. 35;
Popperfoto/Jamil Bittar Reuters: p. 50; Popperfoto/Michael Probst Reuters: p. 4; Popperfoto/
Reuter/Bettmann: p. 36; Popperfoto/Vitaly Armand: p. 47; Rex/Rob Steerwood: p. 30.

Cover photograph of a soldier in Hanoi, Vietnam, reproduced with permission of
Masterfile/R. Ian Lloyd. Background image reproduced with permission of istockphoto.com/
Kristen Johansen

Our thanks to Christopher Gibb and Stewart Ross for their comments in the preparation of
this book.

Disclaimer
All the Internet addresses (URLs) given in this book were valid at the time of going to press.
However, due to the dynamic nature of the Internet, some addresses may have changed, or
sites may have changed or ceased to exist since publication. While the author and publishers
regret any inconvenience this may cause readers, no responsibility for any such changes can
be accepted by either the author or the publishers.

Contents

Any words appearing in the text in bold, **like this**,
are explained in the glossary.

Two Walls

In November 1989, amid scenes of great joy and excitement, the high and heavily fortified wall that divided the communist and Western halves of Berlin was torn down by the people of that city. Since it was built in 1961, the Berlin Wall had offered stark proof of the brutality of **communism**. It was a prison wall, built to prevent people from leaving communist East Germany for the greater freedoms and opportunities of the West. Nearly 100 people had been shot dead trying to escape through its tangles of barbed wire.

A German youth uses hammer and chisel to collect a souvenir of the Berlin Wall, several months after its fall in November 1989.

The wall had divided Berlin, but it had also symbolized the division of the whole world into communist and **capitalist** blocs or areas. The destruction of the wall in 1989 marked the end of European communism as a global power, the end of a 70-year experiment that had clearly failed.

Seven hundred miles to the east, in Moscow, another long wall surrounded the centuries-old fortress of the Russian Kremlin, which for all of those 70 years had been the nerve center of world communism. The graves of ex-communists killed in the early years of the 1917 **October Revolution** could be found along the stretch of wall facing Red Square. A majority were Russian, but there were also representatives from many other parts of the world—men and women who had come to fight and die for what they believed was a new beginning in the human story.

One was the American John Reed, a journalist who witnessed the October Revolution firsthand, wrote an account of it in a famous book called *Ten Days That Shook the World*, and became a founding member of the American Communist Party. Communism, he said, was one of the "most marvelous adventures" mankind had ever set out on.

In the 70 years that separated the beginning of Reed's adventure from the gleeful demolition of the Berlin Wall, communism came to rule one-third of the world, and the struggle to contain it often obsessed much of the other two-thirds. What was it? How did the communist system work—politically, economically, culturally? How did the communist states deal with each other and the rest of the world? What were communism's successes and why, in the end, did it fail? How did a "marvelous adventure" turn into a murderous wall?

Ideas and Ideals

The word communism came from the French word *commun*, which can be translated as "belonging to all." The idea, if not the word itself, has a long history. Centuries before there were communist parties or communist countries, there were people who believed in the simple idea of sharing the ownership and use of society's wealth equally among all its members. This, they thought, would lead to a fairer, kinder society, one in which cooperation and harmony would replace competition and conflict. People would give what they could and take back what they needed.

The Greek **philosopher** Plato thought that such a society would bring out the best in people. So did many of the early Christians. When the 16th-century English political and religious leader Sir Thomas More described a perfect society, or *Utopia*, in his book of that name, he imagined people living communally, sharing their property, and working under the direction of people who had the good of the whole community at heart.

A dream that might come true

Until the late 18th and early 19th centuries this vision was held only by a few isolated individuals. But two great revolutions—the Industrial and the French—changed all that. The **Industrial Revolution**, which began in the United Kingdom, uprooted millions of people, driving them from the countryside into overcrowded towns, where they worked long hours in often terrible conditions. The **French Revolution** showed that a society could be turned upside-down, that the rich and powerful could be successfully challenged. As the Industrial Revolution strengthened the desire for change, so the French Revolution encouraged people to believe that such change was possible.

In the early 19th century the word **socialism** first appeared; like communism later in the same century, it described a society built around the shared ownership of wealth. Some utopian socialists, like Etienne Cabet in the United States and Robert Owen in the United Kingdom, set up model communities—complete villages or small towns—in which people lived according to socialist principles, sharing work and property.

These, however, only affected a small number of people. Most of the new socialists lived in the wider society, where they argued and campaigned for a fairer world. Socialism, communism—whatever this fairer society based on shared ownership was called—was beginning to seem like a dream that might come true.

For details on key communists, see pages 59–60.

A view of New Lanark, the model community founded in Scotland by Robert Owen in the early 19th century.

Karl Marx

One man did more than any other to strengthen this feeling. Karl Marx was a German philosopher and economist, born in 1818, who lived most of his life in England. He was very aware of the unfairness that characterized the newly industrialized countries in the mid-19th century—the huge gap between rich and poor, the appalling conditions under which many people, including many children, worked for such poor rewards. He wanted to make things right, and he thought, like many others through the centuries, that the best way to do so was through the creation of a socialist or communist society.

A statement of intentions

"Let the ruling classes tremble at a Communistic revolution. The proletarians [workers] have nothing to lose but their chains. They have a world to win. 'WORKING MEN OF ALL COUNTRIES, UNITE!'"

(The final lines of *The Communist Manifesto*, written by Karl Marx and Friedrich Engels in 1847–1848.)

But there was a big difference between Marx and his socialist predecessors. They wanted a socialist society, but Marx went further. Through years of study and the writing of many books, he proved to his own satisfaction that a socialist society was actually inevitable, whether one wanted it or not.

According to Marx, the entire human history was a history of struggles between ruling classes (those who owned the wealth and had most of the power) and downtrodden classes (those who did most of the work, but had little power). He thought that throughout history each ruling class—each group of people who dominated a society through either force or wealth or a combination of the two—inevitably created their own opposition. In his time the capitalists—the owners of industry, banks, and communications—were the ruling class in the most advanced countries. To make their world work they needed a growing army of ordinary workers. Marx believed that these workers would eventually get so numerous and so fed up with making wealth for other people that they would kick out the capitalists, confiscate their wealth, and rule in their place. Society as a whole would then own what had previously been owned by a few individuals. Since the workers by this time would make up almost the entire population, their rule was bound to be **democratic**.

Marx had many arguments to back up his prediction of this coming revolution, but he was less certain of what would come after it. He feared that the old rulers would still prove dangerous for a while, and during this period—which he called the dictatorship of the proletariat—the newly victorious workers might have to restrict the old rulers' freedoms. This need would soon pass, however, and society would then enter its socialist phase.

Here Marx distinguished between socialism and communism. Under socialism there would be shared ownership, but people would still be rewarded according to how much work they did. Only when there was enough of everything to go around—a situation which Marx, like many 19th-century thinkers, thought would soon arise—would society move into its final perfect stage: communism. Under communism people would give what they were able to give and take what they needed. There would be no conflict, no need for states or armies or police forces. There would be equality between races and sexes. People would live in natural harmony.

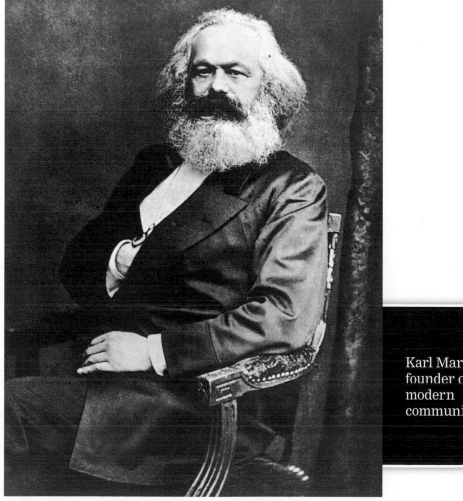

Karl Marx, the founder of modern communism.

Millions of followers

Marx's theories convinced many. During the final decades of the 19th century, Marxist political parties were formed around the world. Students like Vladimir Ilyich Ulyanov in Russia—who, as Lenin, would become the first leader of a Marxist revolution—devoured Marx's writings with excitement and anticipation. They all shared Marx's heady mixture of idealistic hope and absolute certainty; they all believed that both right and history were on their side.

Vladimir Ulyanov at the age of 25, six years before he adopted the name Lenin. After many years of exile in Siberia and western Europe, he led the second Russian Revolution of 1917 and was one of the key figures in building the world's first communist state.

Taking Power

Throughout the 20th century, people who believed in Marx's vision of progress toward communism came to power in many countries. The ways in which they seized control differed widely. In Russia in 1917, workers and soldiers loyal to Lenin's **Bolshevik** Party (later called the Communist Party) simply seized control of the country's major cities and fought a long **civil war** to win control of the countryside. In China Mao Zedong's communist soldiers fought a 20-year civil war against both Chinese and foreign opposition to win power in 1949. This pattern was largely repeated in the countries of Indochina—Vietnam, Laos, and Cambodia—between 1945 and 1975.

For details on key communists, see pages 59–60.

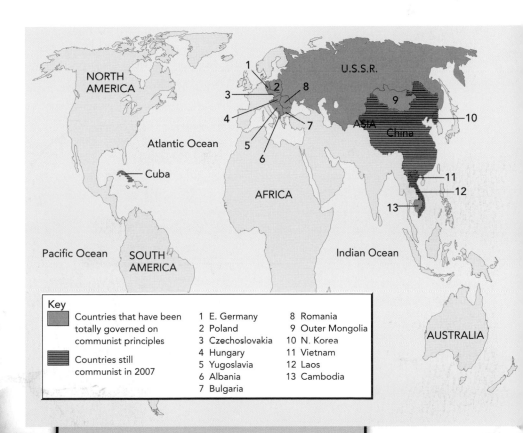

Key

Countries that have been totally governed on communist principles

Countries still communist in 2007

1 E. Germany
2 Poland
3 Czechoslovakia
4 Hungary
5 Yugoslavia
6 Albania
7 Bulgaria
8 Romania
9 Outer Mongolia
10 N. Korea
11 Vietnam
12 Laos
13 Cambodia

Communist states: past and present.

The communist revolution in Russia

There were two revolutions in Russia in 1917. In February* the Tsar was overthrown and replaced by a provisional (temporary) government; in October* that government was overthrown by the Bolsheviks, a Marxist party led by Vladimir Ilyich Lenin. Other prominent members of the Bolsheviks were Leon Trotsky, who organized the armed uprising, and the future leader Joseph Stalin. The Bolsheviks renamed themselves the Communist Party, and for the next 70 years Russia was known as the Union of Soviet Socialist Republics (USSR) or Soviet Union.

*Calendar changes mean that these revolutions may also be dated March and November.

In Yugoslavia, Albania, and North Korea the communists led the resistance to German, Italian, and Japanese occupying forces during World War II, and seized power when those forces withdrew at the war's end. As the **Cold War** began, the **Soviets** (as the Russians were now called) handed over power to the local communist parties in those east European countries they had occupied during World War II—Poland, Czechoslovakia, Hungary, Bulgaria, Romania, and the eastern zone of Germany. In Cuba a group of largely non-communist revolutionaries that had seized power in 1959 were converted to communism by a combination of American hostility to their reform policies and Soviet help. In 1970 the Chilean communist party was actually voted into power in a general election.

Most of these takeovers had a great deal of popular support, and for a very simple reason—they offered at least the promise of turning dreadfully unfair societies into fairer ones. The Bolsheviks, at the time they seized power, had just received the most votes in the new democratic councils or Soviets. Their policies of withdrawing Russia from World War I and giving land to the **peasants** were supported by a majority of the population. In China, the communists, unlike their enemies the **Guomindang,** appeared as a party of honest men who could unify and modernize the country. In Indochina, North Korea, Cuba, Yugoslavia, Albania, and Chile, communists were seen by many as the group that would rescue their countries from foreign occupation or domination.

Only in eastern Europe were the communists largely unpopular from the beginning, and then mostly because they were seen as agents of a foreign power—the Soviet Union.

How Marx thought it would happen, and how it did

In the end neither the manner of the communist takeover nor the level of popularity that the communists enjoyed was what counted. What really mattered were the circumstances in which they took power, and the fact that these were never the circumstances that Marx had considered appropriate for the building of socialism and communism.

Soldiers of the July 26 Movement in Cuba displaying weapons captured in their war to overthrow the dictator Fulgencio Batista.

Marx and his followers believed that history unfolded in an orderly manner. Socialism could only take over from capitalism when capitalism had developed its full potential, and had created an advanced industrial economy, turning most of the population into industrial workers. Marx believed that after seizing power this majority of workers, with their collective, sharing way of working, would take over the enormous wealth created by capitalism and build the socialist society that would one day become a communist paradise. Such revolutions had to happen in the most industrialized countries: the United States, Germany, the United Kingdom, and France.

By the time of Marx's death in 1883, however, it was becoming apparent that things were not going according to plan. Capitalism continued to generate ever-increasing amounts of wealth and, contrary to Marx's expectations, those in power in the advanced countries made sure that a share of the increase went to the poorest members of society. The gap between capitalists and workers remained, but it was not getting wider and wider. Everyone was getting richer, the poor included. Over the next 30 years the introduction of pensions for retired people, unemployment pay, and other benefits in countries like Germany and the United Kingdom improved conditions for the workers even more.

Capitalism was proving much more flexible than Marx had expected, and his followers in these countries found that there were fewer people in favor of revolution. Capitalism continued to create wealth, and the lives of workers could be improved even more within the existing system, particularly now that **trade unions** and democratic politics offered more peaceful ways to press for change. In Germany, which had the largest Marxist socialist party in the world, a clear majority of Marx's followers were, by the beginning of the 20th century, arguing that they could make the world a fairer place without a revolution. Their decision to take the "parliamentary path to socialism," to try to get elected as a socialist, was eventually followed in all the most developed countries.

In other countries, such as Russia, the opposite was happening. Capitalism had barely begun to develop the economies in these countries; there was no majority working class, and no enormous wealth with which to build socialism. Added to this, there was little attempt to improve the conditions of the poor, no democratic government to listen to their complaints, no possibility of peaceful change. In these societies, the communists' call for revolution grew more popular as the 20th century unfolded, and became virtually irresistible once the miseries of World War I had been added to the mix.

Round peg and square hole

In 1917 the first Marxist revolution finally happened in Russia, but not in the way that Marx had imagined. Instead of a dominant, majority working class taking over a country wealthy enough to build socialism, a party representing a small working class took over a largely peasant country. Russia had hardly been developed by capitalism, let alone made ready for socialism.

This was absolutely crucial. By seizing power in backward Russia, Lenin and the Bolsheviks were committing themselves to a project that Marx, their inspiration, would have considered impossible. Trying to build socialism in Russia was like trying to force a large round peg into a small square hole, and the Bolsheviks, in their attempt to do so, would destroy both the peg and the hole. A bunch of **idealists** would end up creating one of the most oppressive regimes in history, and their dream of a fairer society would turn into a nightmare.

Even at the time, the Bolsheviks knew the risk they were running, but they gambled on receiving help from other revolutions in those countries like Germany, where Marx had said socialism would be possible. But no other revolutions succeeded, and Russia—or the Soviet Union, as it was now called—remained isolated and alone.

There was a parting of the ways for the inheritors of the long socialist/communist tradition. Those in the advanced Western countries who had decided to follow the peaceful, parliamentary route to socialism would, from this point on, mostly be known as socialists or social democrats. Those who supported Lenin and the Bolsheviks in opting for revolution in a country obviously unprepared for the building of socialism, would be known as **Marxist**-Leninists—after Marx and Lenin—or simply communists. They would create the systems of political and economic power that we now know as communism.

Workers in Russia's far eastern city of Vladivostok march in support of the revolution in 1922.

Keeping Power

Inside the new Soviet Union, the Communist Party claimed to represent the industrial working class, but this formed only a small minority of the population. Outnumbered by enemies and potential enemies, the Party had no chance of ruling with popular support. Instead, it had to choose between two uncomfortable options: giving up power altogether or establishing a **dictatorship**.

End and means

If the communists had followed their own principles they would have given up power. According to Marxist theory, Russia needed the type of capitalist development that had happened in western Europe before it could embrace the socialism that they were promising. Perhaps not surprisingly, however, none of the leading communists were in favor of stepping aside.

There were several reasons for this. The first might be described as human nature. Having seized power and then defended it at such a cost through four years of bloody civil war, it was asking a lot to expect that they would then simply walk away. And if they did give up power, who could they give it up to? Would they give it to the people they had spent their

White Russian (anti-communist) troops in Siberia during the Russian Civil War, 1919.

whole lives fighting? These were the people who would bring back all the old unfairness; the people who would take the greatest pleasure in having them all shot.

The second reason for their reluctance to give up power was more troublesome. They said they were democrats at heart, that their eventual goal was an utterly democratic paradise, but during the long years of struggle—years on the run or in hiding, years in jail or Siberian exile—Lenin and his fellow communists had acquired distinctly dictatorial habits. They had become more like an army than a party. All the important decisions were made by a small group at the center and handed down as orders. The civil war made this trend worse—by 1921 the communists were used to ruling undemocratically.

These were not, of course, the reasons the communists themselves gave for their dictatorial rule. They justified it as a temporary necessity. If Marx was right, and they believed he was, then history was on their side. They had only to hold out for a few years—until help from other revolutions or their own economic development made socialism and democracy possible in the Soviet Union. If holding out meant that they had to act against their better instincts, then they were prepared to do so. They told themselves that the end (a communist paradise) justified the means (the temporary loss of democracy). They told themselves that they were building an undemocratic bridge into a democratic future.

This idea—of holding political power dictatorially while building up a country's wealth for a socialist future—became the very essence of communism. As the decades went by, the temporary fix became permanent. The dreams of a fairer, freer, more creative society—which, for a few short years after 1917, seemed to promise so much—slowly but surely gave way to intolerance, harsh rule, and **conformism**. These negative characteristics would come to describe communism, not the ideals which had originally inspired it.

For details on key communists, see pages 59–60.

Nikolai Bukharin, a communist Russian leader in the 1920s. He was eventually denounced and executed by the man who became the dictator, Stalin.

The Soviet example

In the wake of the Russian Revolution, communist parties sprang into existence around the world. As in Russia, many of those who rushed to join these parties were idealists who wanted to fight for a fairer world. However, the Soviet domination of the international communist movement meant that most of these idealists soon became infected by the negative characteristics of the Soviet example. Once other communist parties came to power—in China, North Vietnam, North Korea, and eastern Europe—they found themselves facing the same problem the Soviet communists had faced in the 1920s: how

How the power crushed the dream

"In pursuit of their dream the **Bolsheviks** had built up an immense and centralized machine of power to which they gradually surrendered more and more of their dream: proletarian [workers'] democracy, the rights of the small nations, and finally their own freedom. They could not dispense with power if they were to strive for the fulfilment of their ideals; but now their power came to oppress and overshadow their ideals."

(Historian Isaac Deutscher, explaining the dilemma in which the Soviet communists found themselves. They needed power to make their political dreams come true, but in order to stay in power they had to sacrifice those dreams.)

to build an advanced socialist society in a peasant country. They automatically decided on the same undemocratic solutions.

This natural inclination was reinforced by Soviet pressure. The Soviet way of doing things had become the way things were supposed to be done by Marxist-Leninists, the new party line. The Soviet leadership did not want its people to get the impression that there was another, better road to socialism than the one they were currently on. Therefore, any offers of Soviet help to these new communist governments was on condition that they followed the Russian example in all the ways that mattered.

The One-Party State

The communist belief that history was on their side, that mankind was inevitably heading for a communist future, was deeply undemocratic. To the communists, it meant that anyone who disagreed with them was either misguided or motivated by selfish interests; to allow either group a say in the way society was run would obviously be harmful to society as a whole. In some communist states, other parties were allowed to exist, but never to have any real power. These parties were there to make the system look more democratic, not to introduce any real democracy.

Theory and practice

The same logic was applied to democracy inside communist parties. During the early years of the Russian Revolution, democratic debate and decision-making continued to exist inside the Soviet party, but by the mid-1920s factions (or groups) inside that party had been banned on the grounds that they were opposition parties in all but name. By the 1930s the idea of a fixed party line or policy, which all members had to agree to, had been firmly established. Once this line had been decided it had to be obeyed by everyone, both inside and outside the party.

Who decided it? Almost anyone who wished to do so could join the party. In theory, party members all over the country voted members onto local committees. These committees voted members onto the party's Central Committee. The Central Committee elected a small executive group or cabinet, usually called the **Politburo** or Praesidium, to implement its decisions. Policy suggestions and ideas were supposed to be passed up this chain of command; decisions and instructions were to be passed down.

In practice, all real power was concentrated at the center. Local party members relied on people further up the political chain for their jobs, their promotions, and various privileges, and they were reluctant to rock the boat in any way.

Similarly, those in the Central Committee relied on those in the Politburo for their positions and prospects. The Politburo members controlled the center of economic power and the police and armed forces. In the most extreme cases, those in the Politburo relied on one man, who had managed to concentrate all power in his own hands, for their advancement, sometimes even their survival. Lenin's successor Joseph Stalin in Russia, Mao Zedong in China, and Kim Il Sung in North Korea were in this position for long periods, and were, for all intents and purposes, pure dictators. They and they alone took all the crucial decisions which affected their countries.

For details on key communists, see pages 59–60.

The opening Congress of the Communist International or **Comintern**, March 1919.

The role of the secret police and army

The Russian Revolution was only a few months old when Lenin created the **Cheka** (later known by various other names, such as the NKVD, GPU, and KGB). This political police force was supposed to defend a revolution fighting for its life against a wide range of violent political enemies, and many hoped that once that fight was won it would be disbanded. However, the communists, though victorious in the Russian civil war, remained a small minority, and once they had made the decision to establish their (supposedly temporary) dictatorship, they could not risk eliminating the political police.

A strong political police force would become a key feature of the communist system in all the communist states, responsible for both spying abroad and security at home. At best, such forces helped the leadership keep in touch with what people were thinking; at worst, under Stalin, they became instruments of terror, holding entire countries in the grip of fear.

Felix Dzerzhinsky, head of the Cheka, the political police force set up by the Russian communists in late 1917 to defend their revolution.

They also kept an eye on the armed forces. Leaders of military units were teamed with political commissars, party officials who made sure that the party line was being obeyed. In China and Vietnam, where communist armies had led the revolution, this was less necessary. In China during the **Cultural Revolution**, Mao Zedong relied on his supporters in the People's Army to help him overcome opposition to his policies from other party leaders.

The denial of human rights and corruption

In reality, the system concentrated power in only a few hands, which was bound to invite abuses. In theory communist leaders had to answer to party Central Committees, but in reality they were usually only accountable to their own consciences. They were above the law, and could, within very wide limits, do whatever they liked.

This poster shows Mao Zedong promising rich harvests and technological progress in the Great Leap Forward, a program that in fact led to famine and great suffering for the Chinese people.

在共産黨和毛主席領導下，把中國建設成
爲一個繁榮富强的社會主義工業化國家！

They could make major decisions, like Stalin's to restructure Soviet agriculture in 1928, or Mao's to launch the Great Leap Forward in 1958, which would result in millions of unnecessary deaths, without fear of retribution or even criticism during their lifetime. Ordinary people had no **human rights**, only those rights that the party leadership permitted them.

At lower levels, the system invited less serious abuses of power. Party members had access to special shops, special housing, and trips abroad. The party became, in every way that really mattered, a new ruling class. Its members did not own industries or huge properties, but they had the use of them, which amounted to the same thing. The party official in charge of an automobile factory could get cars for his party friends, all of whom were doing similar favors connected with their own work.

As the years went by, any lingering idealism gradually gave way to widespread **cynicism** and **corruption**. Communist parties originally formed to serve the people slowly turned into private clubs designed to serve only their members. Without democracy, without the chance to say no to this state of affairs, there was no hope of changing it.

Rosa Luxemburg

The Polish communist Rosa Luxemburg was one of the leaders of the German Spartacus League, which became the German Communist Party in 1918. She was a great believer in democracy, and warned the leaders of the Russian Revolution what would happen if they abandoned democracy. The life would be sucked out of all public institutions, she said, leaving government in the hands of a few dozen party leaders and a large, unfeeling bureaucracy. There would be a "brutalization of public life."

Luxemburg herself was murdered during the German communist uprising of January 1919.

The Planned Economy

The central feature of socialism and communism was the shared ownership of what Marx called the means of production, those things that allowed goods to be made and distributed—such as the factories, tools, and transportation systems. Immediately after seizing power in October 1917, the Soviet communists took these away from the private individuals who had owned them and made them the property of the state. Their intention was to run them for the good of the whole population, rather than for the profit of their owners.

During the civil war that followed the communist takeover, the economy collapsed, money virtually disappeared, and people relied on barter (simple exchange) to get what they needed to live. Some communists believed that this was true communism in action, but Lenin knew that such a situation could not last. The people of the new Soviet Union were simply sharing their poverty. True communism was about sharing wealth. The key responsibility of the party was to develop the Soviet Union, to make it richer.

The key decision

Lenin's New Economic Policy (NEP), introduced in 1921, was designed with this in mind. The peasants, who formed the vast bulk of the population and who had been given the land they worked by the new communist government, were encouraged to produce more food, make more money, and spend it on **industrial goods**. This, it was hoped, would stimulate industrial expansion and cause the entire economy to grow.

The plan only worked slowly, however, and other drawbacks soon became apparent. The party needed peasant support, but at the same time it was unwilling to share this power with anyone, let alone those they considered the least-educated part of the population. Also, the NEP looked more like a return to capitalism than progress toward socialism. Many in the party preferred the idea of taking control of the whole economy, and of adopting a harder line toward the countryside.

For details on key communists, see pages 59–60.

If the peasants were paid less than the **market rate** for their crops, they argued, then the difference could be invested in industrial expansion and the growth of the whole economy speeded up. In the late 1920s these men, led by Stalin, won the argument and launched what was effectively a second revolution, introducing the **collectivization of agriculture** and central planning of industry.

Soviet dictator Joseph Stalin cultivated a kindly 'Uncle Joe' image to cover his cruel and ruthless policies.

Collectivization

Not surprisingly, many peasants preferred eating their surplus crops to selling them at a low price. The Soviet party, left with the choice of accepting a slow rate of growth or taking complete control of the countryside, chose the second. The peasants resisted, and many millions died as a result. Many were shot by the political police, and many more died through mistreatment in the labor camps of the frozen north, but the vast majority died in the famines that followed the peasants' wholesale destruction of their own animals and crops. Despite the resistance, nearly all of the Soviet Union's privately owned farms had been gathered into huge collective farms by 1932. The farmers became paid workers, and their harvest now belonged to the state. There was some good in this—collective farms, for example, could afford modern equipment that individual farmers could not—but it was vastly outweighed by the bad. Most people in the countryside never forgave the party for the horrors of collectivization, and few tried to make it work.

Collectivization—the human tragedy

"'I am an old Bolshevik,' the GPU [Gosudarstvehnoye Politicheskoye Upravlenie—the political police] Colonel said, almost sobbing.
'I worked in the underground against the Tsar and then I fought in the civil war. Did I do all that in order that I should now surround villages with machine-guns and order my men to fire indiscriminately into crowds of peasants? Oh, no, no!'"

(A Soviet official contrasting his and the revolution's hopes with the terrible reality of collectivization.)

Male and female workers threshing grain on a collectivized farm near the town of Mariupol in the Ukraine, a country that became part of the Soviet Union in 1922.

In China, the leadership tried to soften the blow by introducing collectivization a little bit at a time, hoping to persuade the peasants as they went, and it was only in 1958 that the Communes—even larger versions of the Soviet collective farms—were finally set up. Enthusiasm was high at first, and there were significant successes, but in the end the Communes proved as much of a failure as the Soviet collective farms. In the early 1980s, they were divided up into small plots for peasants to rent.

Centrally planned industry

In the Soviet Union's state-owned industry and agriculture, each individual unit—whether factory or farm—was told what it was expected to produce over a given period of time. The central planners in Moscow decided where the units should get their raw materials, how much the workers should be paid, to whom they should sell their products, and at what price. Every unit's plan was included in a national plan that covered a five-year period.

At first this system worked well. Planning the expansion of basic industries like steel was not a particularly complex task: the number of different products was small, the work mostly unskilled, the calculations relatively simple. The Soviet economy in the 1930s, as measured by the production of such basic items, grew at a remarkable speed. So did those **developing world** economies that adopted the Soviet system after World War II. As a system of basic industrial development, communism was an economic success, and arguably no more inhumane than capitalism during the horrors of the original Industrial Revolution.

Of course such levels of planning led to further restriction of freedoms. People could not change jobs or move to new areas when they wanted to, because the plan relied on them staying and working where they were. But there was some compensation for this loss of freedom—a guarantee of work for everyone. During the Great Depression of the 1930s, when millions of people were unemployed in the capitalist countries, this seemed one of communism's real advantages.

How industry was planned

If, for example, the central planners decided that a new tractor factory should be built in Siberia, they needed to arrange a supply of steel for the construction of the tractor bodies. For the extra steel to be manufactured, they needed to arrange the mining of extra coal and iron. Both these materials would require transporting, which would involve the building of extra trains, which would create the need for even more steel. Extra workers with the right skills would need to be assigned to each operation, and they would need housing, schools for their children, and other facilities. The planners had to make all these calculations for every sector of the economy, and see that they were all in balance with each other.

The steelworks at Anshan, part of China's drive for industrialization in the 1950s.

The Totalitarian Society

Communist states went to great efforts to convince their citizens that the party line on any particular subject, the official view or explanation, was the right one. This was partly because, in most cases, they believed that this was so, but it was also because they were unwilling to tolerate any opposition to either the party's way of doing things or its vision of the future. This type of society, one that demands complete obedience to the state and allows only one way of seeing things, is usually called **totalitarian**.

Education, media, and arts

Education was given a high priority in communist states, and in non-political subjects, such as science, the standard was often very high. In subjects with an obvious social or political relevance, the bias was much more evident. History, economics, and politics were only taught from a Marxist point of view, and at times of crisis—as, for example, in China during the Cultural Revolution— these were virtually the only subjects taught.

There were no privately owned media in communist countries, and major newspapers such as *Pravda* in Russia and the *People's Daily* in China simply reflected the current party line on those issues the party considered important. Radio—and later, TV—did the same. Few different points of view were expressed in news

Attacking the past

"Red Guards all over China took to the streets, giving full vent to their vandalism, ignorance, and fanaticism. They raided people's houses, smashed their antiques, tore up paintings and works of calligraphy [artistic handwriting]. Bonfires were lit to consume books. Museums were raided. Palaces, temples, ancient tombs, statues, pagodas [temples], city walls—anything old was pillaged."

(Jung Chang in her autobiographical novel ***Wild Swans***, describing what happened after Mao Zedong launched a nationwide campaign to destroy the four olds: old ideas, old culture, old customs, and old habits.)

shows or plays, and there was a tendency to fill broadcasting hours with essentially non-political subjects like chess, science, and sports.

There was an explosion of artistic creativity during the early years of the Russian Revolution: the poets Mayakovsky and Esenin, the film-maker Eisenstein, and the architect Tatlin were only the best known among many figures of international importance. However, the closing down of free debate soon infected the arts, and by the end of the 1920s artists were being ordered to use their work to promote the party line. This style, which dominated communist arts for the next 50 years, was called socialist realism, but it was usually far from realistic. In the Soviet Union, writers produced heroic novels about the struggle to build steel mills in the Siberian wilderness; in China, traveling theater groups told the story of how heroic peasants, inspired by the thoughts of Mao Zedong, had broken all records for grain harvested in a single day.

In later years, as their populations grew less willing to accept such a one-sided view of reality, the communist states allowed artists more freedom, and in some European countries such as the Soviet Union and Czechoslovakia, there was a significant revival of creativity, especially in movies.

For details on key communists, see pages 59–60.

A still frame from Sergei Eisenstein's movie *Alexander Nevsky* (1938). Eisenstein was the best known of the early Soviet filmmakers.

Stalin's head is projected onto clouds above Moscow's Red Square.

Religion and the personality cult

Religion was downplayed by communism. Marx called religion "the opium of the people," by which he meant that it was a drug to keep them from thinking. Most communists considered religion's promise of a heavenly after-life a trick to keep the poor happy on Earth. Although religious worship was rarely banned in communist countries, it was made extremely difficult in most of them over a long period of time.

Meanwhile, the communists turned their own leaders into virtual gods. The first to be given this treatment was the dead Lenin, whose body was embalmed (preserved) and placed in a tomb in Red Square for people to view through the years to come. His writings became like holy books, his picture appeared everywhere. Right up to the end of the Soviet Union, Lenin had a god-like status which he himself would have found laughable.

A similar **personality cult** was created for Stalin while he was still alive. His face covered entire buildings and was even projected onto the clouds. Writers celebrated his "universal genius"; hospitals, rivers, towns, and factories were named after him.

Over the top?

North Korean leader Kim Il Sung was known as Great Leader throughout his more than 40 years in power. Starting in the 1960s, every North Korean adult wore a badge bearing Kim Il Sung's face, and by the late 1980s there were 34,000 monuments to him scattered around North Korea. This number did not include those benches where he had once sat, which were now protected with glass coverings. Kim was followed everywhere by an assistant who wrote down his every word, and citizens were occasionally sent to prison for accidentally sitting on a newspaper bearing his photograph.

After Stalin the Soviet communists stopped building up their leaders in such a way, but elsewhere in the communist world the practice continued. During China's Cultural Revolution, Mao allowed himself to be turned into a virtual god. Millions of people chanted from the famous "Little Red Book" of his sayings. Children were encouraged to believe that "Father is dear, mother is dear, but Chairman Mao is the dearest of all." In North Korea the worship of leader Kim Il Sung was taken to even greater extremes.

Holding back the past

The party outlawed religion partly out of conviction, and partly because it wished to deny people the opportunity of a different viewpoint, of another way of seeing things. The non-communist past also offered a source of comparison, and some communist states tried to discourage their citizens from looking back in time. Generally speaking, Soviet communists had little to fear from comparisons with the Russian past, which was rarely kinder than their own rule—Russia's churches, for example, were not all torn down. But during the Cultural Revolution in China, there was a conscious effort to destroy the past, and much of the country's heritage was lost.

Even this cultural vandalism paled in comparison to what happened in Cambodia, which was renamed Democratic Kampuchea during the rule of the communist group Khmer Rouge (1975–1978). The Khmer Rouge made the decision to erase the nation's memory by executing all those, such as teachers and writers, who carried the knowledge of previous centuries in their minds. The Khmer Rouge said their goal was to restart history with a blank slate at year zero. Almost a third of Cambodia's six million people were killed.

Victims of the Khmer Rouge: a mound of skulls in an abandoned Cambodian schoolhouse.

Opposition

Despite the attempt to impose only one way of looking at things, there was always at least some opposition to communist rule. Many individuals were arrested and jailed, but mass protests were rare, and violent protests even rarer. When violence was used—as, for example, during a revolt by sailors at Kronstadt in the Soviet Union (1921) or the national uprising against Soviet intervention in Hungary (1956)—the rebels were swiftly overpowered. Even when the opposition was peaceful—as it was in Czechoslovakia during the Prague Spring of 1968 and in China during the student protests that ended tragically in Tiananmen Square (1989)—the country's armed forces were called out to crush the protesters.

Most opposition was kept within relatively safe bounds. Writers would circulate political articles and stories among friends, and sometimes smuggle them out to the capitalist world for publication. Ordinary people expressed their disenchantment by cheating the state whenever they could get away with it, and by retreating into family life and leisure. It was often only possible to express one viewpoint in public, but the party rarely interfered with what people thought or said in their own homes.

Tanks of the People's Liberation Army rumble toward a defenseless student in China's Tiananmen Square in June 1989.

Foreign Relations

When it came to dealing with the rest of the world, the new communist governments in the Soviet Union had two contradictory goals in mind. On the one hand, it saw the governments of capitalist countries as its natural enemies, and wanted to help the people of those countries overthrow their governments and replace them with communist ones. They considered it their international duty to promote other revolutions, and as early as 1919 they set up the Communist International (Comintern) to organize a global support network.

Lenin addresses the Second Congress of the Communist International in 1920.

On the other hand, they could not afford to provoke and antagonize other countries to the point where their own revolution was threatened. As the years went by, and priority was given to building up the Soviet economy, the need for trade and foreign technology made it necessary to improve relations, at least on the surface. Some support was still given to revolutionary movements elsewhere, but generally speaking the Soviet communists, convinced that time was on their side, became much more interested in proving that their own system was better at producing economic growth than the capitalist one.

A common enemy

In the 1930s the security of the inward-looking Soviet Union was threatened by the rise of Nazi Germany. Nazism, like Soviet communism, was a totalitarian system that did not tolerate other beliefs, but in other ways the two ideologies were almost opposites. Communists believed in government ownership, science, internationalism, racial, and sexual equality; Nazis believed in private ownership, **romanticism**, **nationalism**, **racism**, and keeping women in the home. Added to this list of fundamental differences was the fact that the Nazi leader Adolf Hitler made no secret of his desire to conquer large areas of the Soviet Union for future German settlement.

The Soviet communist leader, Stalin, did all he could to deflect this threat. He tried to form an alliance with the western powers of Britain and France, but was rebuffed. He then signed the **Nazi-Soviet Pact** with the Germans, in which the two states promised not to attack each other. Stalin hoped that this would provide him with time to rearm the Soviet Union while the Germans were fully occupied in the West. He won himself only two years, but they may have been crucial.

Germany finally attacked the Soviet Union in June 1941, and so for the rest of World War II Stalin found himself in uneasy alliance with the capitalist West. Once the war was over and Nazism had been defeated, the alliance crumbled for the simple reason that the two sides had few shared interests. In eastern Europe, either capitalism or communism had to triumph—there was rarely a middle way. Between 1945 and 1948 the Soviets, worried about future attacks, wanted to make sure that choice was communism. The United States thought this was the first step in a plan of communist expansion, and took hostile measures of their own. For the next 40 years, relations between the United States and the Soviets, between the democratic West and communism, would be marked by suspicion and antagonism.

For details on key communists, see pages 59–60.

This posed photograph shows a **Red Army** soldier hoisting the Soviet flag above the ruins of the German parliament building after the capture of Berlin, May 1945.

The Russo-German Front during World War II (1941–45)

In the months that followed the attack by Nazi Germany on the Soviet Union in June 1941, the Communist army was forced to surrender huge areas of western Russia and the Ukraine. Fortunately, one of the key elements of the first two five-year development plans in the 1930s had been the relocation of many Soviet factories to the east of the country, and the weapons produced in these factories proved crucial in first holding and then driving back the Germans. Through 1944 and 1945 the Soviets faced 90 percent of the German army, while the Western powers in France and Italy faced only 10 percent. Estimates suggest that roughly 20 million Soviet citizens died in World War II, more than those of all other European and North American countries put together.

The Cold War

The threatened use of nuclear weapons, invented in the 1940s, meant that the Cold War never became an actual war. Once the Soviets exploded their own atom bomb in 1949, neither they nor the United States could risk what came to be known as Mutually Assured Destruction (MAD). Both continued to improve the number and quality of their bombs and bomb delivery systems, but neither ever expected to get so far ahead in this arms race that it could risk starting a nuclear war.

Because they did not dare engage in military conflict, the Soviet Union and the United States competed politically and economically. In the 1950s and early 1960s, people in both camps became convinced, mostly because of the Soviets' many achievements in space, that the Soviet economy was catching up with the U.S. economy. It was not until the 1980s that it became obvious that this was never going to happen. In the meantime, the two governments and their allies competed in the developing world for friends and influence. On the communist side, the Russians helped build, projects such as the Aswan High Dam in Egypt, the Chinese built the Tanzam railway in central Africa, and the Cubans offered both military and civilian help—doctors and teachers—to many other developing world countries.

During the half-century that followed World War II, there were many examples of conflicts involving communist parties or armies around the world, but the Russian communists stuck to the decision they made in the 1920s, putting the interests of their own country ahead of helping out fellow communists. They supported the Cubans economically, and they supplied arms to friends like the North Koreans and North Vietnamese, but the only time they became militarily involved in a full-scale war to help foreign communists was in Afghanistan during the 1980s. In this case, their intervention had more to do with concern that the war might spill across the border into their own territories, than with any generosity of spirit.

This Soviet reluctance to support other revolutions was one of the main reasons for the breakdown of the relationship between the Soviet Union and China in the 1960s. At this stage both the Chinese and the Cubans were eager to spread revolution to the rest of the developing world, and

Vietnamese communists open fire on U.S. aircraft attacking their village in South Vietnam, April 1969.

they were angry with the Soviets for refusing to help them. Starting in the early 1970s, however, they followed the Soviet example, preferring their own security and economic well-being to running the risks of supporting world revolution.

Inflexibility and Collapse

The tremendous growth in the Soviet Union's basic industries in the 1930s, and that country's dominant role in the defeat of Nazi Germany in World War II, seemed, for a short while, to back up the communists' claim that they were creating a valid alternative to capitalism. But as the postwar world unfolded, the gap between communist ideals and reality began to grow ever more obvious. There might be economic growth and scientific advances to boast about, but there was little else. Communist society in the Soviet Union, and those that had been created in eastern Europe, were much less free, much less creative, and not noticeably fairer, than the capitalist societies of North America and western Europe. If communism was to mount a real challenge to capitalism, it needed to clean up its act and reform itself.

Khrushchev and the first attempts at reform

The first leader to attempt this was the Soviet leader Nikita Khrushchev, who rose to power after Stalin's death in 1953. He believed that the communist system created by Lenin and Stalin was fundamentally sound, but blamed Stalin for creating the climate of terror that had stifled initiative throughout Soviet society. Khrushchev released some prisoners, stressed collective (joint) leadership, and introduced a few very limited economic reforms. The party's grip was very slightly relaxed.

This had two important consequences. First, the economy remained sluggish—the party's grip was still too tight. Second, even this slightest relaxation produced a challenge to the party's rule. There was no trouble in the Soviet Union, but in both Hungary and Poland the introduction of Khrushchev's very minor measures proved enough, in 1956, to put the entire system in danger. In Poland matters were solved peacefully by a simple change of communist leaders, but in Hungary the Soviet Union had to use tanks to reinstate a government it approved of.

Over the next 35 years, this pattern of events would become a key feature of European communism. The obvious need for reforms

For details on key communists, see pages 59–60.

would push the party into introducing them, but the reforms would end up threatening the party itself. Communism was essentially unreformable.

China

In the 1950s, China went through much the same process that the Soviet Union had been through in the 1930s—heavy industry was expanded through five-year plans and agriculture was collectivized. By the end of the decade, Mao Zedong was growing impatient, and in 1958 he introduced an accelerated program of growth called the Great Leap Forward. This plan, which tried to substitute massive effort and enthusiasm for proper planning, created chaos, especially in the countryside where a resulting famine killed roughly 20 million people between 1959 and 1962.

In 1960, as this disaster unfolded, Mao was forced to hand over control of the economy to moderates Liu Shaoqi and Deng Xiaoping. However, his god-like status as the creator of the revolution meant that he retained a large following in both the party and the country. Liu and Deng got the economy moving again, but Mao believed that they were stressing economic progress at the expense of communist ideals, and taking the party away from ordinary people. In 1966, with the support of the People's Army and the units of enthusiastic young Red Guards, he launched the Cultural Revolution, partly as a way of giving the revolution back to the people, partly as a way of putting himself back in control. Another period of chaos followed, this one lasting almost a decade, in which many millions of people were killed and many more millions had their lives turned inside out.

Officials in dunce caps are paraded through Beijing by Red Guards during the Chinese Cultural Revolution.

The elderly Deng Xiaoping took over the leadership of China after Mao's death in 1976. Under new leadership, the Communist Party kept tight control of the political situation. In 1989, for instance, it used tanks and troops ruthlessly to break up a pro-democracy protest meeting in Beijing's Tiananmen Square. Less spectacularly, however, the party was relaxing its grip on China's economy. Enterprising individuals were allowed to set up and run their own businesses, making money and widening the wealth gap between themselves and the masses. It looked very much like capitalism.

Cuba and Czechoslovakia

Mao was not the only communist who believed that Khrushchev and later Soviet leaders had lost touch with the idealism that had been such an important part of communism's original appeal. In the 1960s, the first decade of the revolution in Cuba, a deliberate effort was made to appeal to people's better, more idealistic nature and less to their greed for possessions. The Cubans also stressed the old communist idea of helping other revolutionaries around the world. Che Guevara, the Argentinian who had been one of Cuban leader Fidel Castro's most important partners in creating and running the revolution, left Cuba to fight for more revolutions in both Africa and South America. He was killed in Bolivia in 1967.

There was also a strong hint of idealism in the events that overtook Czechoslovakia in 1967–1968. These, like the events in Hungary 12 years earlier, grew out of reforms that had been introduced in the Soviet Union, and which then galloped out of control. The Czechoslovaks, under party leader Alexander Dubcek, believed that more democracy would be better in itself, and would also make the economic reforms more effective. They thought the party could control this process, but the Soviets were not prepared to risk their being wrong, and in August 1968 sent in the tanks to stop the experiment.

The system self-destructs

By the 1970s, communism around the world was stuck in a deepening rut. The promise of economic growth, which had once offered some compensation for the absence of freedoms, was rapidly evaporating. The planned economy had worked well as an engine of basic development, but it was becoming obvious that it was unable to deliver the goods in a sophisticated consumer economy. Delivering ten million shoes was one thing; delivering ten million shoes of the various sizes, colors, and styles for 200 million consumers was much more difficult. There were just too many calculations for the planners to make.

Alexander Dubcek, First Secretary of the Czechoslovak Communist Party, and the leader of the 1968 Prague Spring.

Russia's first post-communist leader Boris Yeltsin (left) shares a word with the last leader of the Soviet Union, Mikhail Gorbachev.

Meanwhile, increased exposure to international sporting events and increased cultural contacts gave the Soviet people a better idea of what life was really like in the West, and this increased the pressure for greater freedom in politics, the arts, and life in general. Radical reform was becoming inevitable, but until 1985 the party still feared introducing it. Then Mikhail Gorbachev took over as leader, and finally introduced the wholesale changes that had been needed for so long.

As the party had always feared, real reform led to collapse. Gorbachev could not carry through his policy of *perestroika* (restructuring of the system) without fatally weakening the power of the Communist Party, and between 1988 and 1991 the party lost the ability to impose its will on eastern Europe, the non-Russian areas of the Soviet Union, and finally Russia itself. A far from perfect democracy took over from one-party rule, and free enterprise replaced the planners. By 1991 there was not a communist state left in Europe.

Power to the people

"The essence of **perestroika** is for people to feel they are the country's master."

(Mikhail Gorbachev in 1986, explaining that the party must become more democratic.)

Communism in the 21st Century

Fifteen years after the collapse of the Soviet Union, communist parties still held power in several countries, but there were many who doubted whether any of these countries could still be considered truly communist.

As we have seen (page 45), the prime example of these semi-communist countries was China. The government realized that a state-controlled economy could not compete with a capitalist one, and saw that economic failure had been the main reason for the collapse

Shanghai's Oriental Pearl Tower and Jin Mao Tower are soaring symbols of China's new capitalist enterprise.

The gospel according to Deng

"It does not matter whether a cat is black or white as long as it catches mice."

(Chinese leader Deng Xiaoping in the 1980s, explaining that the party was willing to consider any methods of achieving economic growth, no matter how uncommunist they might be.)

of the USSR. To keep the same thing from happening in China, it opened the Chinese economy to market forces. In the short term, this diverted attention away from political reform.

The situations in Vietnam and Cuba were similar: in both countries the ruling parties tried to invigorate their economies by enlarging the role of market forces without relinquishing overall political control, to introduce a measure of capitalism without introducing democracy. In Cuba, the government enjoyed significantly more support than in other communist countries, for a number of reasons. The revolution's undoubted successes, particularly in health and education, were attributed to the government, while many of its failures were rightly blamed on the U.S. policy of refusing to trade with Cuba for 40 years. Whether the regime's popularity would survive the death of its founder Fidel Castro remained an open question.

Developing world prospects

The developing world at the beginning of the 21st century was full of countries bearing all the characteristics of Russia in 1917—mass poverty, great unfairness, and economies dominated by foreigners and small local elites. Given this, the possibility that political parties promising increased development, greater fairness, and strict controls on foreign business might gather support and seize power was far from remote. A sign of this happened in Venezuela, where the popular Hugo Chavez launched what he called a socialist revolution in 2005. Something similar looked as if it might happen in Nicaragua, where in 2006 the left-wing Daniel Ortega was reelected president.

If such 21st-century communists did seize power, they would encounter enormous problems. They would face the same dilemmas as the Bolsheviks had a century before them: to abandon power or to abandon democratic principles; to develop at a snail's pace or on the backs of an unwilling peasantry. Whichever decisions they took, the economic difficulties and human cost would be great.

For details on key communists, see pages 59–60.

Another force favoring communist-style government was at work, too. This was the threat of massive climate change, brought about by the pumping of millions of tons of carbon dioxide into the atmosphere. Many experts blamed capitalism for this situation: for decades companies and individuals had been so eager to increase their wealth that they had forgotten or ignored the effect this was having on the

Cuba's President Fidel Castro in September 2001. Castro, who came to power after leading a revolution to victory in 1959, is one of the world's longest-serving leaders.

Anti-communism in action

"Not a nut or a bolt will be allowed to reach Chile under Allende . . . We shall do all in our power to condemn Chile and the Chileans to utmost deprivation and poverty, a policy designed for a long time to come to accelerate the hard features of a communist society in Chile."

(Edward Korry, U.S. Ambassador to Chile, correctly predicting what his country would do in the event of a victory for the communist coalition led by Salvador Allende in the Chilean election of 1970.)

environment. One answer, it was suggested, was for governments to take more control over industry and force it to cut emissions of carbon dioxide. Government control of industry was, of course, a central plank of communist teaching.

In the developed world

In ex-communist European countries, the old communist parties lingered on with varying degrees of success. In those which were adapting better to capitalism—like the Czech Republic—communism was rarely more than a bad memory, but in those like Russia, where the transition was proving a painful process, people sometimes tended to forget communism's bad points and remember the good. Rising unemployment and rising levels of crime made them hunger for the old job security and law and order of Stalin's day.

In the developed countries of North America and western Europe, the communism of Lenin and Stalin never came to power, either peacefully or through revolution. These were the countries that Marx had believed would follow the path he mapped out through revolution, the dictatorship of the working class and socialism, to the promised paradise of communism. For most of the time, the capitalism of the **free market** held undisputed sway. After the collapse of European communism at the end of the 1980s, capitalism's victory seemed complete.

For all its successes and strengths, capitalism faced mounting problems as the 21st century advanced. Critics noted that the emphasis on what the English poet William Wordsworth called "getting and spending" was undermining society by encouraging selfishness and materialism. Hatred of what they saw as the godless West was one reason for the growing Muslim **terrorism**. Then there was the danger of global warming, which some claimed as the price of capitalism's triumph. In the end, therefore, a more sharing society may be needed, one that might even look slightly communist. It is quite certain, however, that it will not look anything like the communism that played such a large role in the history of the 20th century.

So, What Is Communism?

Communism was (and, in some small parts of the world, still is) that system of political, economic, and social organization that spread across one-third of the world from its birthplace in Russia. Communist takeovers were often fueled by idealism, but this was soon swept aside by the practical necessities of producing economic growth in previously backward economies. The system that evolved to meet this challenge in Russia during the 1920s and 1930s became the model for all the other communist countries to follow, at least in their early years. It is this system which we now associate with the much older word communism.

The system had several key features. Only one political party—the Communist Party—was allowed to hold real power. Decisions within this party were generally taken at the highest levels and passed down as instructions or orders. Ordinary people had a few limited ways of making their feelings and thoughts known to the leadership, but it was not a democratic system in any true sense. The political police played crucial roles in keeping the party informed about what the people were thinking, and in clamping down on any anti-government activity.

Another key feature—many would say the central defining feature of communism—was the creation of an almost completely government-owned economy, in which almost all activities were planned in advance. This economic dictatorship was intertwined with the political dictatorship, to the point where neither could be reformed without the other.

Crushed hopes

"We revolutionaries, who aimed to create a new society, 'the broadest democracy of the workers,' had unwittingly, with our hands, constructed the most terrifying State machine conceivable; and when, with revulsion, we realized the truth, this machine, driven by our friends and comrades, turned on us and crushed us."

(Russian revolutionary Victor Serge, writing in the 1940s.)

Other facets of social life—such as education and sports, the arts, and the media—were controlled by the party, and used to advertise and promote the party's version of reality. Communist achievements and capitalist failures were taught and reported; communist failures and capitalist achievements were rarely mentioned. In some communist countries, a personality cult was built around individual leaders that took this blatant disregard of truth even further. There was, in these instances, a clear intention to create an almost religious atmosphere. The communists were doing exactly what they had criticized the churches for doing—offering a god and a wonderful future in return for a terrible life in the here and now.

The traditional May Day celebration in Moscow's Red Square, 1954.

Why it lasted so long

Although it limited individual freedom and often brought great hardship, communism still had millions of supporters. In many cases, communist states seemed to be an improvement over previous ruling parties. Lenin's Soviet Union, Mao's China, and Castro's Cuba were no less democratic than the regimes that they replaced, and seemed to offer much more to the majority of ordinary people. Furthermore, not all the favorable comparisons were with the past. Cubans, for example, compared themselves with other Latin Americans, and though many resented Castro's dictatorial ways, they also took pride in having better healthcare and higher literacy rates than their capitalist neighbors.

In the Soviet Union, communism was bolstered by national pride in the country's superpower status. In countries such as China, Vietnam, and Cuba, a central feature of the communist takeover was the expulsion of foreign influence, and success in this regard sparked an upsurge in national pride that was slow to fade. In eastern Europe the opposite was the case—communism's association with Soviet domination made it even more unpopular than it would otherwise have been.

An experiment that failed

It is hard to exaggerate the impact of communism in the 20th century. It inspired many with its vision of the future, and condemned many more to hardship and suffering. Much the same could, of course, be said of its great enemy, capitalism, over the last two centuries. What really distinguished communism was the enormous gulf that developed between the theory and the practice, the promise and the reality. There were substantial communist achievements in the fields of basic economic development and science, but in most communist countries these were eventually outweighed by later economic stagnation and the loss of democracy.

The disciples of Marx and Lenin who set out to make the world a better, fairer place for everyone ended up creating one of the least efficient, least democratic, and least humane systems in modern history. Communism's failure and the reasons for it should be understood and remembered, but so should the fact that millions of people around the world once thought it a cause worth fighting and dying for.

It remains to be seen what will happen to the communist societies in existence today.

Shortages of bread and other essentials were common in the Soviet Union, but they continued even after the end of communism in Russia, as this photo taken in 1991 shows.

Communism and capitalism

"What is the difference between capitalism and communism? Capitalism is the exploitation of man by man; communism is the reverse."

(A popular saying in Poland during the years of communist rule, which expressed the widely held belief that the two systems were as bad as each other.)

For details on key communists, see pages 59–60.

Timeline

1818	Birth of Karl Marx, Trier, Germany
1848	Marx's and Engels' *Communist Manifesto* published
1867	The first volume of Marx's key work *Capital (Das Kapital)* published
1883	Death of Karl Marx
1898	The Marxist Russian Social Democratic Labor Party (RSDLP) is founded
1903	The RSDLP splits into Bolshevik and Menshevik factions
	Birth of Mao Zedong
1905	During a year of rebellion the first soviets appear in Russian cities
1914–18	World War I
1917	The first communist revolution takes place in Russia
1918–21	Russian civil war
1919	Formation of Comintern (or Communist International)
1921	Kronstadt rebellion
	Lenin introduces the New Economic Policy
	Foundation of Chinese Communist Party
1924	Death of Lenin
1927	Trotsky exiled
1928	Stalin introduces the first five-year development plan
1929–33	Soviet collectivization of agriculture
1934–35	The Long March of the Chinese Communist Party
1934–38	Stalin's campaign of violence and intimidation within the Soviet Union
1939–45	World War II
1941	Nazi Germany attacks the Soviet Union
1945–48	Countries of eastern Europe forced to accept communist governments
1947	Cold War begins
1949	Founding of the People's Republic of China
1950–53	Korean War
1953	Death of Stalin
1954	France expelled from Vietnam by communists
1956	Khrushchev attacks Stalin in a secret speech
	Soviet troops crush the Hungarian rebellion
1958	Mao launches the Great Leap Forward

1959	Cuban revolution
1961	Construction of the Berlin Wall begins
1964	Khrushchev is forced out by his colleagues
1966	Mao launches the Cultural Revolution
1967	Che Guevara captured and murdered in Bolivia
1968	Prague Spring in Czechoslovakia Soviet and other allied armed forces invade Czechoslovakia
1970	Communists win election in Chile
1973	Military coup topples the communist government in Chile
1975	Vietnam is reunited as a communist state Khmer Rouge take over in Cambodia
1976	Death of Mao Zedong
1978	Deng Xiaoping introduces far-reaching reforms
1979	Sandinista (communist) victory in Nicaragua Vietnamese invade Cambodia to overthrow the Khmer Rouge Soviet Union invades Afghanistan in support of its communist government
1985	Gorbachev takes over as Soviet leader
1989	Pro-democracy demonstrations in Beijing are crushed by troops Eastern Europe abandons communism Fall of Berlin Wall
1991	Soviet Union breaks up; Gorbachev resigns
1997	Death of Deng Xiaoping
1999	Cuba's Fidel Castro celebrates 40 years in power
2001	China joins the World Trade Organization
2003	Hu Jintao replaces Jiang Zemin as president of China
2005	Venezuela's elected president, Hugo Chavez, begins breaking up large estates as part of his socialist revolution
2006	Communist North Korea tests a nuclear device Ex-communist Daniel Ortega returns to power in Nicaragua

Further Information

Further reading

Downing, David. *Leading Lives: Vladimir Ilyich Lenin.* Chicago Heinemann Library, 2002.

Downing, David. *Leading Lives: Josef Stalin.* Chicago: Heinemann Library, 2002.

Orwell, George. *Animal Farm.* New York: Penguin, 2003.

Ritchie, Nigel. *Communism.* New York: Raintree Steck-Vaughn, 2001.

Ross, Stewart. *The Collapse of Communism.* Chicago: Heinemann Library, 2004.

Stewart, Whitney. *Deng Xiaoping: Leader in a Changing China.* Minneapolis, Minn.: Lerner Publishing Group, 2001.

Taylor, David. *The Cold War.* Chicago: Heinemann Library, 2002.

Websites

These sites deal with communism and its history:

www.gmu.edu/departments/economics/bcaplan/museum/musframe.htm

www.bbchistorymagazine.com/linkread.asp?id = 13125

Video: http://video.google.com/videoplay?docid = 47280569076693147631

For information on individual countries, perhaps start with Russia:

http://members.aol.com/TeacherNet/Russia.html

and China: http://library.thinkquest.org/26469/history

Key Communists

Fidel Castro (1927–) led the July 26 Movement in Cuba which, in 1959, overthrew the dictator Fulgencio Batista after a short guerrilla war. Castro announced that he had become a communist in 1961, and has led Cuba ever since.

Deng Xiaoping (1904–1997) was one of the more moderate leaders of the Chinese party in the 1950s and early 1960s. Disgraced during the Cultural Revolution, he was brought back to repair the economy in the 1970s, and served as the real leader of China from then until his death.

Friedrich Engels (1820–1895) was Marx's friend and intellectual partner. He co-wrote *The Communist Manifesto* and wrote several important works of his own.

Mikhail Gorbachev (1931–) took over the leadership of the Soviet Union in 1985 and introduced far-reaching reforms that ultimately undermined the power of the party, the unity of the country, and his own position. He resigned in 1991.

Ernesto "Che" Guevara (1928–1967) was an Argentinian who took part in the Cuban guerrilla uprising led by Fidel Castro. He served in the Cuban government for several years, but then left Cuba to assist revolutions in central Africa and Bolivia. He was caught and murdered in 1967.

Ho Chi Minh (1890–1969) founded the Indochinese Communist Party in 1930, and became the communist president of North Vietnam in 1954. From 1959 until his death he supported the South Vietnamese communists in their struggle against a U.S.-supported government.

Kim Il Sung (1912–1994) led the armed resistance to the Japanese occupation of Korea in the 1930s and 1940s, and became leader of Soviet-occupied North Korea in 1945, a position which he held until his death.

Vladimir Ilyich Lenin (1870–1924) was the leader of the first Marxist revolution, the second Russian Revolution of 1917. Leader of the Bolshevik wing of the Russian Social Democratic Labor Party since 1903, he persuaded his party to seize power.

Mao Zedong (1893–1976) was a founding member of the Chinese Communist Party in 1921, and its leader from the mid-1930s. After the communist victory in 1949 he supervised the construction of a Soviet-style economy and tried to accelerate growth through the 1958 Great Leap Forward. This failed, but in 1966 he launched the Cultural Revolution against party bureaucracy. This proved another disaster for Chinese economic development, and in the last years of his life, Mao was once again forced to share power with his more moderate colleagues.

Karl Marx (1818–1883) was the German philosopher, economist, and political scientist whose theories of social development helped to inspire both socialism and communism. He was active in politics, and a founder of the First International, an association of trade unions of different countries.

Pol Pot (c.1925–1998) was the leader of Cambodia's Khmer Rouge regime in the late 1970s. His policies of reconstruction were responsible for some two million deaths.

Joseph Stalin (1878–1953) became General Secretary of the Soviet party in 1921, and used that position to rid himself of potential opponents. By the end of the 1920s, when he launched the five-year plans and the collectivization of agriculture, he was the country's undisputed dictator. In the 1930s he created a climate of terror in which millions of people were imprisoned or killed, but he proved a competent military leader during World War II.

Leon Trotsky (1879–1940) organized the actual uprising in October 1917 and led the Red Army to victory in the civil war. After Lenin's death he unsuccessfully opposed the rise of Stalin. He was exiled in 1927 and finally murdered by an agent of Stalin in 1940.

Glossary

Bolshevik one of the two political parties that emerged from the 1903 split in the Russian Social Democratic Labor Party. Bolshevik is Russian for "those with a majority."

capitalism economic system in which the production and distribution of goods depend on private wealth and profit-making

capitalist someone who owns capital (money or property), and combines it with other people's labor to make profits

Central Committee after 1917, the committee elected by local Communist Party committees throughout the Soviet Union. This in turn elected a smaller ruling committee, the Politburo.

Cheka the Extraordinary Commission for Combating Counter-Revolution and Sabotage: the political police force created by Lenin in December 1917

civil war war between different groups in one country

Cold War name given to the hostility that existed between the free enterprise capitalist and communist worlds between 1947 and the late 1980s

collectivization of agriculture creation of large, jointly-owned farms by joining together small farms that had previously been privately owned

Comintern the Communist International, an organization formed by the world's communist parties with the goal of promoting world revolution

conformism going along with the existing customs or rules; not wanting to rock the boat

corruption immoral practices like bribery or fraud

Cultural Revolution decade of political chaos and instability in China, unleashed by Mao Zedong, with the support of the Red Guards and People's Army, in 1966. Mao's goal was to weaken those in the party who wished to follow a Soviet-style policy of economic progress at the expense of grassroots involvement. The conflict was not resolved until after Mao's death in 1976.

cynicism tendency to expect the worst from people

democracy political system in which governments are regularly elected by the majority of the people, or a country in which this system exists

developing world poorer countries of the world

dictatorship government by an individual (called a dictator) or a small group that does not allow the majority of the people any say in their government

embargo policy of not trading with a particular country

fascism dictatorial system of government originating in Italy, which was later known for its aggressive nationalism. Nazism was one type of fascism.

free market economy in which individuals rather than governments make the decisions about which goods and services are produced, and how they are bought and sold

French Revolution political upsurge in France that began with the storming of the Bastille prison in 1789, and developed into an assault on the upper classes, ending with the execution of the King and many aristocrats in the 1793–1794 reign of terror.

Guomindang (Kuomintang) Chinese nationalist movement led by Chiang Kai-shek which lost to the communists in the Chinese Civil War

human rights rights that should belong to any person

idealism belief that the world can be made a better place

industrial goods goods made from raw materials or other goods made in factories or workshops

Industrial Revolution change from a primarily agricultural economy to one based on large-scale production in factories that began in England in the 18th century

market forces workings of supply (what is or is not available) and demand (what is or is not wanted)

market rate price that a buyer and seller would agree on if there was no intervention from government

Marxism ideas of Marx and his followers

nationalism active promotion of national interest, often at the expense of humanity as a whole

New Economic Policy (NEP) reintroduction of limited private trading after the Russian Civil War

October Revolution second Russian Revolution of 1917 that brought the communists to power

orthodoxy usual way of doing things

peasant farm worker or owner of a small farm

personality cult campaign of exaggerated praise for an individual leader

philosopher thinker about life

Politburo Soviet cabinet (or small ruling committee elected by the Central Committee)

racism belief that individuals or groups are inferior because they belong to a different race than your own

Red Army army formed by the Bolsheviks to defend their revolution in the civil war

revolutionary in politics, working to overthrow the entire existing order

romanticism philosophy that considers emotion more important than thought

socialism set of political ideas that puts more emphasis on the needs of the community as a whole and less on the short-term wants or needs of the individual

Soviet Russian for council

terrorism use of violence to achieve political ends

totalitarian form of society demanding obedience to one set of political, social, and cultural ideas

trade unions organizations formed to protect and advance the pay and conditions of workers

Index